MW00565028

1⦿-MINUTE
GAME and GADGET
PROJECTS

BY TAMMY ENZ

CAPSTONE PRESS
a capstone imprint

Dabble Lab is published by Capstone Press, an imprint of Capstone.
1710 Roe Crest Drive, North Mankato, Minnesota 56003
www.capstonepub.com

**Library of Congress Cataloging-in-Publication Data is available
on the Library of Congress website**
ISBN 978-1-4966-8090-7 (library binding)
ISBN 978-1-4966-8094-5 (eBook PDF)

Summary: Need entertaining game and gadget projects for your
makerspace? You've come to the right place! From spy gadgets and
marshmallow cannons to bubble blowers and mini bowling alleys, these
amazing 10-minute projects will have kids making in no time!

Photo Credits
All photographs by Capstone: Karon Dubke; Marcy Morin and
Sarah Schuette, Project Production; Heidi Thompson, Art Director

Design Elements
Shutterstock: best_vector, casejustin, Dr Project, Epine, Fafarumba,
Jaws_73, keport, mijatmijatovic, newelle, sergio34, strizh, Tukang
Desain, vectopicta

Editorial Credits
Editor: Christopher Harbo; Designer: Tracy McCabe;
Media Researcher: Tracy Cummins; Production Specialist: Katy LaVigne

All internet sites appearing in back matter were available and accurate
when this book was sent to press.

TABLE OF CONTENTS

GOT 10 MINUTES?

If you like making games and inventions, look no further. With a few simple supplies you'll be taking target practice, solving codes, and lighting up your world in no time. Best of all, these super-fast projects will leave you with plenty of time to test them out and clean up afterward!

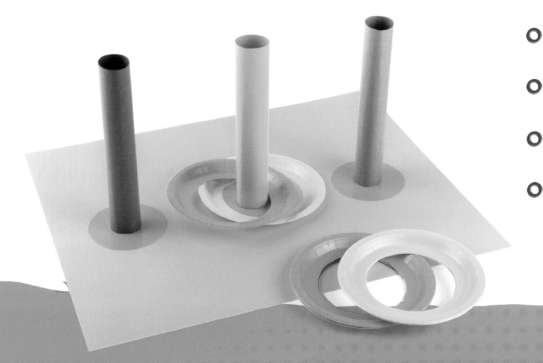

General Supplies and Tools

balloons
bottle caps
chopsticks
clothespins
construction paper
contact paper
craft sticks
disposable cups
electrical tape

hammer and
   nails
hot glue gun
markers
measuring cups
pencil
poster board
rubber bands
ruler

scissors
screwdriver
stapler
straws
string
tape
utility knife

Tips

- Gather all of your supplies before starting a project.

- There's no right or wrong way to make these projects! Experiment and use your imagination.

- Ask an adult to help you with sharp or hot tools.

- Add your own flair! Make each creation unique by adding your own ideas.

MARSHMALLOW TARGET SHOOT

What can you do with marshmallows, a balloon, and a few common supplies? Whip up this cool game that can be played anywhere.

What You Need:

disposable cup
utility knife
balloon
scissors
1 sheet of construction paper
tape
marshmallows

What You Do:

1. Ask an adult to cut out the bottom of the cup with the utility knife.

2. Tie the open end of the balloon in a knot. Snip off the other end of the balloon with the scissors.

3. Stretch the snipped end of the balloon over the cup's bottom. Wrap the balloon around the sides of the cup.

4. Cut a piece of construction paper in half lengthwise. Tape the two halves end-to-end to make a long strip.

5. Loop the strip of construction paper into a circle and tape it together to make a hoop.

6. Set the hoop on the floor. Stand about five paces away. Place a marshmallow in the cup and pull back the balloon's knot. Release the knot to launch the marshmallow into the hoop.

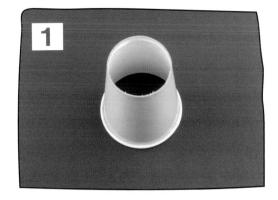

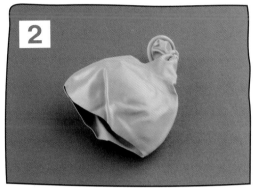

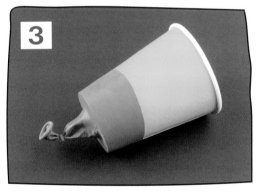

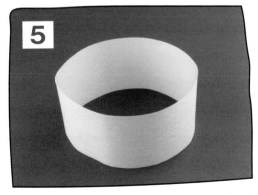

TIP Make several hoops of different sizes. Give each a point value and then test your skill at shooting into the hoops.

CANDY LAUNCHER

Clothespins can do more than just hang your laundry. Harness their power to make a launcher that can shoot candy across the room!

What You Need:

- clothespin
- small block of wood
- hot glue gun
- craft stick
- utility knife
- ruler
- bottle cap
- candy

What You Do:

1 Take a clothespin apart. Then turn the spring around and place it backward on one half of the clothespin.

2 Center the flat side of the clothespin on the block of wood. Hot glue the clothespin in place.

3 Ask an adult to use the utility knife to carve a notch about 0.5 inch (1 cm) from the end of the craft stick.

4 Slide the craft stick into place so the notch is under the spring.

5 Hot glue the bottle cap to the other end of the craft stick. Leave the last 0.25 inch (0.6 cm) of the stick showing so you can push on it.

6 Place a small candy in the cap. Push the stick down as far as possible. Release the stick to send the candy flying.

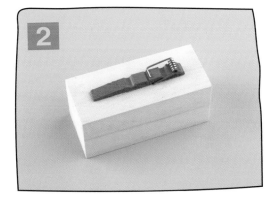

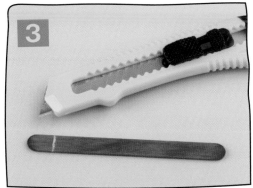

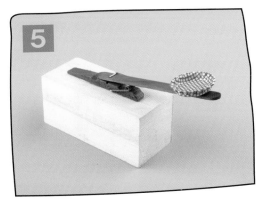

TIP Use your launcher to fling other small objects, such as beads, coins, or tiny toys.

9

LOOP HOOPS

How good is your hand-eye coordination? Test it out with a classic game you can build yourself.

What You Need:

marker
mini disposable cup
orange table tennis ball
nail
hot glue gun
18-inch- (46-cm-) long piece
    of string
chopstick

What You Do:

1. Draw lines on the table tennis ball and the cup to make them look like a basketball and a hoop.

2. Punch a hole in the bottom of the cup with the nail.

3. Glue the ball to one end of the string. Thread the other end of the string through the bottom of the cup. Tie a large knot on the end of the string.

4. Push the tip of the chopstick into the bottom of the cup. Glue it in place.

5. Holding the chopstick, swing the ball up and try to catch it in the cup.

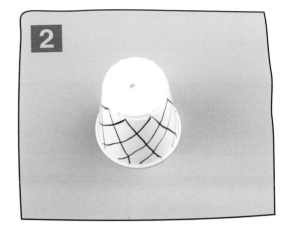

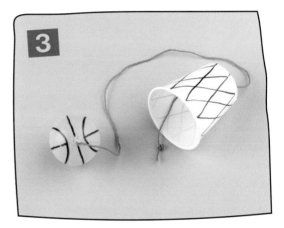

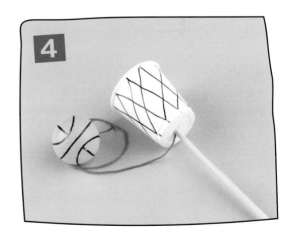

TIP To increase the challenge, try attaching a longer string to the ball and cup.

11

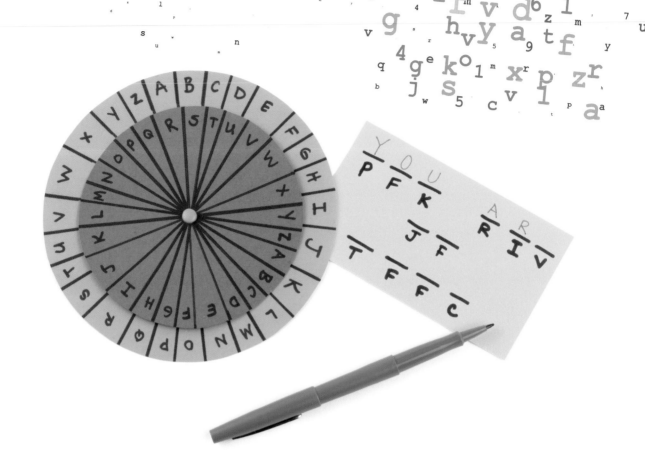

CIPHER WHEEL

Protect your secret notes from prying eyes.
Build a cipher wheel to send and solve coded
messages between friends.

What You Need:

construction paper

CD

cereal bowl

marker

scissors

ruler

brass fastener

pencil and paper

What You Do:

1 Place the CD and the cereal bowl, face down, on the construction paper. Trace around both objects and cut out the circles.

2 Mark the center of the small circle. Place a ruler on this mark and draw a line to divide the circle in half.

3 Make 12 equally spaced marks on each half of the circle. Use the ruler and marker to connect these marks by drawing lines through the center of the circle. Label each section from "A" through "Z."

4 Stack the small circle on the large circle. Connect them in the center with a brass fastener.

5 Extend the lines of the small circle onto the large circle. Label these sections "A" through "Z" too.

6 Write a message on a piece of paper. Spin the circles so like letters don't line up. Code the message by replacing each letter used from the large circle with the letter it's next to on the small circle.

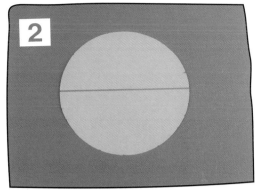

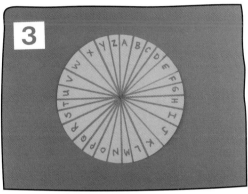

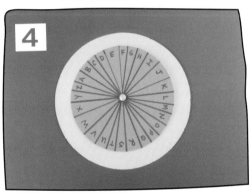

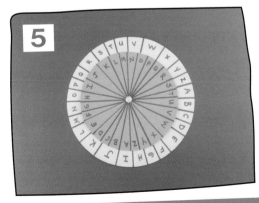

TIP Help friends decode your messages by telling them which letter on the small circle lines up with the A on the large circle.

13

CELL PHONE AMP

Don't let a small cell phone speaker spoil your dance tunes. Make this handy amp to pump up the volume!

What You Need:

marker
paper towel tube
2 sheets of construction paper
scissors
2 disposable cups
tape
utility knife

What You Do:

1. Trace around one end of the tube on a piece of construction paper. Cut out the circle and tape it to the side of a cup. Make sure the circle sits about 0.5 inch (1 cm) from the bottom of the cup.

2. Ask an adult to cut around the circle with a utility knife. Remove the tape.

3. Repeat steps 1 and 2 with the other cup.

4. Roll the other sheet of construction paper around the tube and tape it in place. Stick the ends of the tube into the holes in the cups.

5. Ask an adult to cut a slit on the top of the paper towel tube with a utility knife. Make the slit just large enough to fit a cell phone.

6. Slide your phone into the slit and play some music.

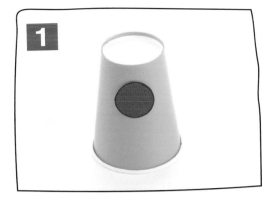

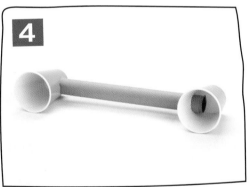

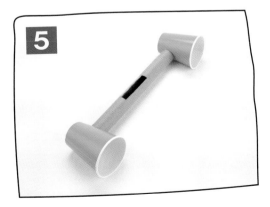

MINI FLICK FLASHLIGHT

This mini flashlight is powerful, easy to make, and holds a secret. Just a flick of the wrist will turn it on.

What You Need:

small tin box
hammer and nail
mini LED bulb
electrical tape
CR2032 button battery
mini tilt switch
wire clip
hot glue gun

What You Do:

1 Use the hammer and nail to punch a hole in one end of the box. Make the hole large enough to fit the tip of the LED bulb.

2 Tape the long leg of the LED to the positive (+) side of the battery.

3 Tape one of the tilt switch legs to the negative (-) side of the battery.

4 Clip the short leg of the LED to the remaining leg on the tilt switch. Tilt the circuit back and forth to see the LED light up.

5 Place the circuit in the box so the LED shines out of the hole. Glue the battery to the bottom of the box.

6 Close the box. Flick the box up or down when you need a flashlight.

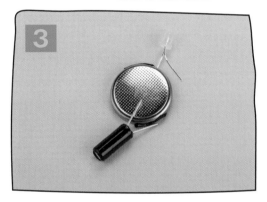

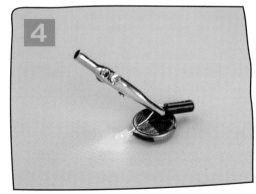

TIP Tilt switches and LEDs can be found at most hobby stores and electronics shops.

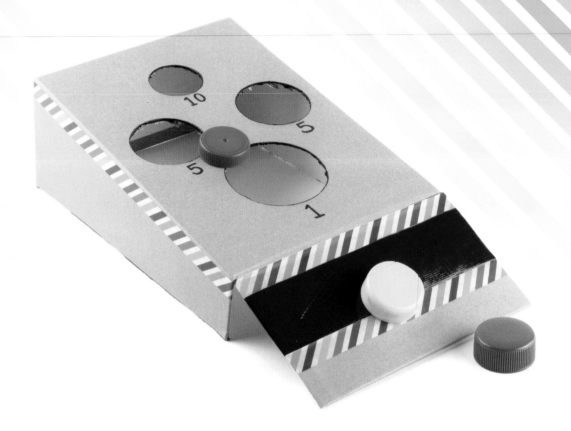

BULL'S-EYE SHOOTER

No festival or fair is complete without a Skee-Ball game. Now you can whip up this mini version to play on the go.

What You Need:

- shoebox
- ruler
- marker
- scissors
- small bowl
- small cup
- milk cap
- water bottle cap

What You Do:

1 Open the flap on one end of the box.

2 Use the marker and ruler to draw a diagonal line from the middle of the open end to the corner of the closed end. Cut along this line.

3 Repeat step 2 on the other side of the box. Set the box facedown so it looks like a ramp.

4 Place the bowl, cup, milk cap, and water bottle cap on the ramp. Trace around each object, then remove and cut out the circles.

5 Label all of the circles with points. Give the large circles small point values and the small circles large point values.

6 Place the water bottle cap at the bottom of the ramp. Flick it with your finger to try to make it go into an opening. Add up your score after five tries.

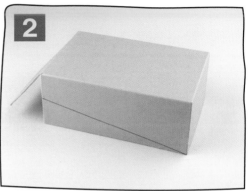

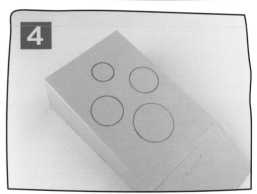

TIP Flick the cap from different angles to try to hit different holes.

BALLOON
HOVER GAME

Here's a game that will leave you breathless.
See how long you can keep a balloon hovering
with lung power!

What You Need:

disposable cup   bendable straw
ruler   hot glue gun
pencil   balloon
scissors

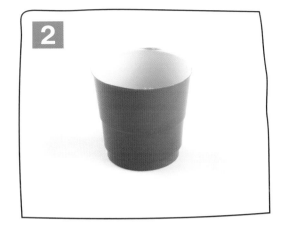

What You Do:

1. Measure 1.5 inches (4 cm) from the bottom of the disposable cup. Draw a line around the cup at this mark.

2. Cut along the line. Discard the top of the cup.

3. Poke a small hole in the bottom of the cup with the scissors.

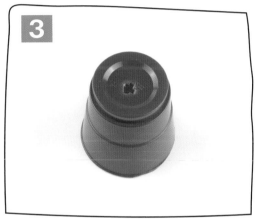

4. Bend the straw and stick the short end into the hole. Glue around the straw inside the cup to hold it in place.

5. Blow up the balloon and tie it closed.

6. Set the balloon on the cup. Blow into the straw to make the balloon hover.

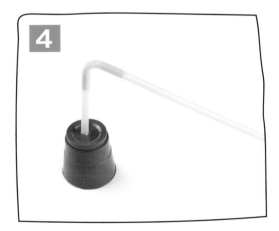

TIP Make a pair of hover balloons. Then challenge a friend to see who can keep a balloon in the air longer.

TIC-TAC-TOSS MAT

Give a game of tic-tac-toe a clever twist.
Make a giant game board and fling
plastic lids as X's and O's.

What You Need:

ruler

clear contact paper

9 10-inch (25-cm) squares of poster board (two colors)

scissors

10 plastic lids (two colors)

What You Do:

1 Cut one 31-inch- (79-cm-) long strip of contact paper. Lay it on a flat surface sticky side up.

2 Place three poster board squares on the contact paper, alternating the colors. Leave a 0.5-inch (1-cm) gap between them.

3 Repeat steps 1 and 2 with two more strips of contact paper and the remaining poster board to create a checkerboard pattern.

4 Cover the top of the squares with three more 31-inch- (79-cm-) long strips of contact paper. Trim off any extra edges.

5 Place the mat on the floor and challenge a friend to a game of tic-tac-toe. Stand 10 steps away from the mat and take turns flinging the plastic lids. The first person to connect three squares in a row wins!

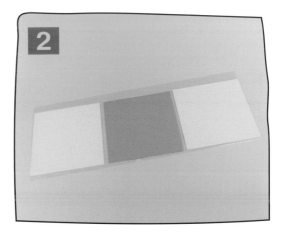

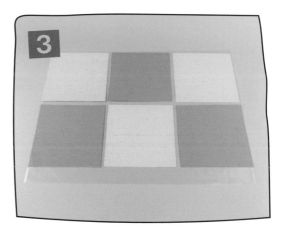

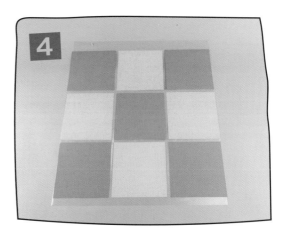

GIANT BUBBLE BLOWER

No summer is complete without a little bubble blowing. Take your bubbles to the next level with this nifty gadget.

What You Need:

plastic bottle
utility knife
1/8 cup (30 mL) dish soap
1/8 cup (30 mL) light corn syrup
1 teaspoon (5 mL) glycerin
1/4 cup (60 mL) hot water
bowl
spoon

What You Do:

1 Ask an adult to cut off the bottom half of the bottle with a utility knife. Recycle the bottom of the bottle. Set the top of the bottle aside.

2 Mix the soap, syrup, glycerin, and water in the bowl. Stir slowly with the spoon.

3 Dip the cut edge of the bottle top in the mixture.

4 Blow through the bottle's spout to make giant bubbles.

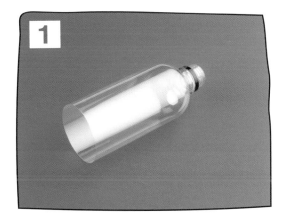

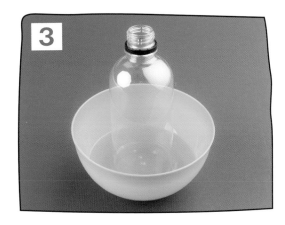

TIP Use this bubble blower outdoors on a breezy day to see the bubbles float up and away.

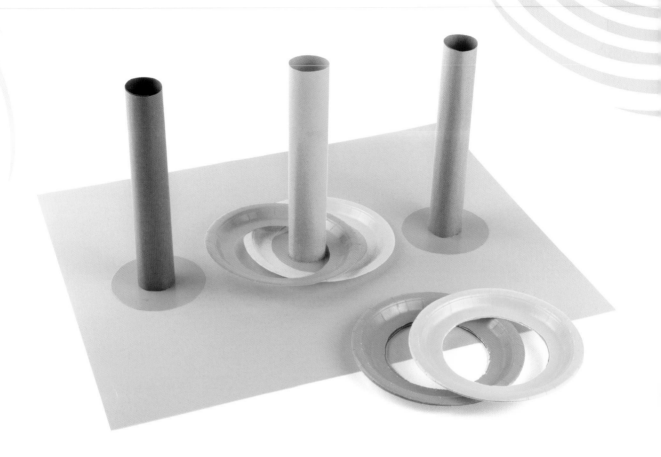

RING FLING

Ring toss is a popular party game. Make your own version in minutes with just a few simple supplies.

What You Need:

3 sheets of construction paper, each a different color

tape

hot glue gun

1 sheet of poster board

10 paper plates (two colors)

scissors

What You Do:

1 Cut the center out of each paper plate. These are your rings.

2 Roll each sheet of paper into a tube about 2 inches (5 cm) wide. Tape the edges of each tube to hold it in place.

3 Glue the tubes to the circles cut from the paper plates in step 1.

4 Glue the circles and tubes to the poster board. Place them about 12 inches (30 cm) apart.

5 Place the game board on the floor and take 10 steps back.

6 Give a friend five rings of the same color. Take turns tossing them at the tubes.

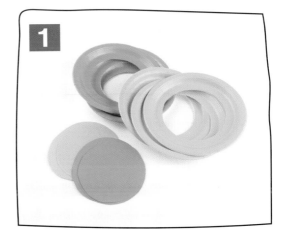

TIP Assign points to each tube. For instance, one point for the closest tube, two points for the middle tube, and three points for the farthest tube.

KNOCK
HOCKEY

Clear off a table or desk! With just a couple of goals and some chopsticks, you'll have your very own hockey rink.

What You Need:

12 bendable straws
hot glue gun
2 water bottles
milk cap
2 chopsticks

What You Do:

1 Bend two straws into 90-degree angles. Glue their long sides together to make a goalpost. Repeat this step with a second pair of straws.

2 Slide a straw between the goalposts to make a crossbar. The crossbar should sit about 5 inches (13 cm) above the bent legs of the goalposts.

3 Adjust the legs of the goalposts so the goal stands by itself.

4 Repeat steps 1 through 3 to make another goal.

5 Place the goals on opposite ends of a table. Stand water bottle goalies 2 inches (5 cm) in front of each goal.

6 Set the milk cap "puck" in the center of the table. Take turns flicking the puck with a chopstick to try to shoot it through the goalposts.

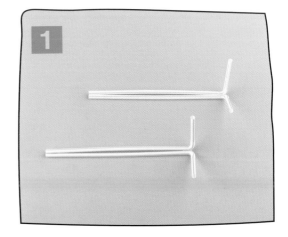

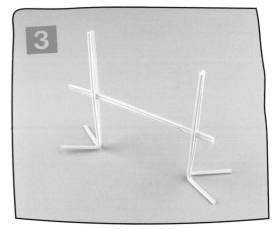

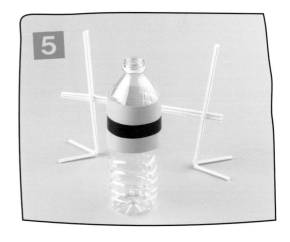

TIP Make up your own rules! What happens if you hit the puck off the table without going through the goal? Maybe your opponent gets two shots in a row from the middle of the table.

29

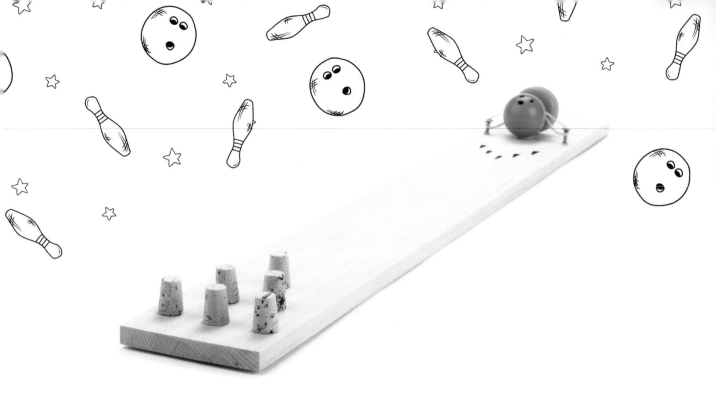

MINI BOWLING ALLEY

Bowling is a game of skill and determination.
See how your game measures up with this
easy-to-make mini alley.

What You Need:

- 24-inch- (61-cm-) long board
- 2 1-inch- (2.5-cm-) long drywall screws
- screwdriver
- milk cap
- hammer and nail
- 6-inch- (15-cm-) long rubber band
- table tennis ball
- markers
- 6 corks

What You Do:

1. Lay the board flat. Screw the drywall screws into the board about 4 inches (10 cm) from one end. Place each screw about 0.25 inch (0.6 cm) from each side of the board. Screw them in only halfway.

2. Use the hammer and nail to make two holes in the milk cap. Make the holes about 0.5 inch (1 cm) apart. Thread the rubber band through the holes on the underside of the cap.

3. Adjust the loops so they extend equally from the top of the cap. Place each loop over a screw.

4. Use markers to decorate the table tennis ball with "finger holes" and the board with bowling lane arrows.

5. Place the corks on the other end of the board in a triangle formation.

6. Set the ball between the screws. Draw back the cap and let it go to launch the ball at the pins.

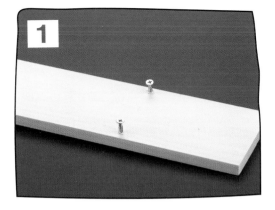

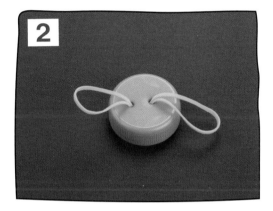

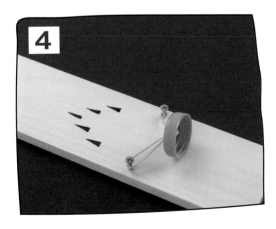

Read More

Challoner, Jack. *Maker Lab: 28 Super Cool Projects: Build, Invent, Create, Discover.* New York: DK Publishing, 2016.

Heinecke, Liz Lee. *STEAM Lab for Kids: 52 Creative Hands-On Projects Exploring Science, Technology, Engineering, Art, and Math.* Beverly, MA: Quarry Books, 2018.

Holzweiss, Kristina. *Amazing Makerspace DIY Movers.* New York: Children's Press, 2018.

Internet Sites

20 Fun and Easy Games for Kids and Adults
www.youtube.com/watch?v=amGarkUgGow

Games Kids Can Make
www.instructables.com/id/Games-kids-can-make/

Make Games and Toy Crafts for Kids
www.artistshelpingchildren.org/gamestoysarts
craftstideaskids.html

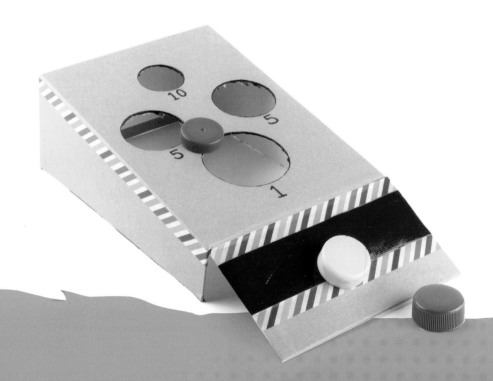